ASTROLOGY

ASTROLOGY

HELEN SUDELL

PHOTOGRAPHS BY MICHELLE GARRETT

LORENZ BOOKS

NEW YORK • LONDON • SYDNEY • BATH

This edition published in 1996 by Lorenz Books,
an imprint of Anness Publishing Limited.
Administrative office: 27 West 20th Street
New York, NY 10011.

Lorenz Books are available for bulk purchase for
sales promotion and for premium use.
For details, write or call the manager of special sales,
LORENZ BOOKS, 27 West 20th Street,
New York, NY 10011. (212) 807-6739.

Produced by Anness Publishing Limited
1 Boundary Row
London SE1 8HP

ISBN 1 85967 272 8

Publisher: Joanna Lorenz
Copy Editor: Beverley Jollands
Designer: Lillian Lindblom
Photographer: Michelle Garrett
Step Photography: Janine Hosegood
Illustrations: Lucinda Ganderton

Printed in Singapore by
Star Standard Industries Pte Ltd

CONTENTS

INTRODUCTION

Which sign were you born under? Whether you scoff at the whole business of astrology, plan your days around it or read newspaper horoscopes in secret, you probably know the answer to that question. Though astrologers would say there is much more to the subject, it is the signs that appeal to most of us.

That the sun and moon govern life on earth is self-evident: the sun is the source of light and warmth, while the moon exerts its pull on the tides and other natural cycles. Looking up to the heavens to observe these life forces, early sky watchers discovered other bodies which they thought might also exert some influence over them: the stars in their fixed patterns, interwoven by the wanderings of the restless planets.

For these early observers of this stately nocturnal dance, the shapes of the constellations were enhanced by leaps of imagination that transformed them into recognizable and familiar things: a beautiful woman, a scorpion, a scuttling crab, a regal lion. The Greek word "zodiac" means a circle of animals, and it came to mean this majestic, fanciful circus, wheeling nightly across the darkened sky.

The Babylonians, Egyptians and Chinese each independently evolved a zodiac as a means of measuring time, dividing the sun's supposed yearly circuit around the earth into sections: the calendar months. The Babylonians devised eighteen signs, including the twelve still in use today. That makes these powerful, well-known images at least three thousand years old.

No one knows the exact origins of the astrological symbols. Looking up at the constellations, you will probably not see a set of scales, a ram or a crab. But the arrangements do provide clues; Gemini has a pair of bright stars that could have suggested twins, and the curving line of stars in Scorpio does look a little like a scorpion's tail.

Top: A late-eighteenth-century sun and zodiac design from the Koloaensky Palace in Russia, which has since been destroyed.

Some symbols are appropriate to seasons on earth, such as Aquarius the water-bearer, who coincides with the winter rains, and Virgo, whose season is high summer and who is identified with the harvest and the seed for next year's corn .

Mithras, a sun god whose worship began in Persia, was enthusiastically adopted by Roman soldiers. They built temples in his honor and his shrines were invariably surrounded by carvings of the signs of the zodiac, which then became known throughout the ancient world. At Roman chariot races, each team started from a stall bearing a star-sign, and Petronius describes a zodiacal feast at which each sign had its appropriate dish: there was beef for Taurus and fish for Pisces, while Libra was represented by a balance with different food placed on each scale. By the second century AD, Roman coins were imprinted with the birth sign of the current emperor, and zodiacs were often worked into the design of sumptuous mosaic floors.

Left: An Egyptian coffin lid showing the signs of the zodiac.

Zodiacs continued to appear as architectural details; astrological signs were carved in Canterbury Cathedral and included in the stained glass of Chartres. A pillar of the Doge's Palace in Venice is crowned by a beautiful capital carved with astrological symbols,

Above: A detail from a fifteenth-century Flemish tapestry of the astrolabe and zodiac, from Toledo Cathedral, Spain.

and the signs were a picturesque component of many fifteenth-century Italian frescoes. They also appear on jewelry, ceramics and furniture.

In the Middle Ages, star-signs were commonly used as illustrations in illuminated manuscripts on a variety of subjects. Richly decorated books of hours naturally included signs as tokens of the passing months. In the outstanding example of this genre, *Les Très Riches Heures du Duc de Berry*, the signs progress around an arching band of stars set above each exquisite miniature of French courtly and peasant life.

In the late sixteenth century, many European thinkers began to reject astrology as superstitious rigmarole at odds with the scientific discoveries of the dawning Age of Enlightenment. However, this did nothing to stop the popularity of almanacs, which had been published widely from the earliest days of printing and continue to be issued today. In the modern world, astrology is not so easily dismissed and is once more a subject of serious study. It has regained its foothold in the popular imagination.

Zodiac signs can be seen everywhere now, from silk scarves to walls and ceilings. Although all are distinctive, some have a pleasing symmetry that makes them satisfying as motifs in an ordered design, while the animals have a special appeal, whether painted, sewn or modeled. Because astrological signs are birth signs, they are obviously a perfect theme for birthday presents, and you will find a host of ideas in this book to inspire you to be especially creative. More subtle and mysterious are the "sigils", or calligraphied symbols, that represent each sign. These stylized shapes, with their bold, flowing lines, make wonderful subjects for techniques such as stenciling. Use the one appropriate to your birth date, or combine them all for a magical effect.

Above: A page from the exquisite Les Très Riches Heures du Duc de Berry, *a fifteenth-century illuminated manuscript illustrated by the Limburg brothers.*

Above: Tiled panel showing Gemini, the twins, with angels playing the flute. From the Palacio dos Marqueses de Fronteira, Portugal.

Each of the twelve signs is associated with one of the four elements which were once believed to be the foundations of the natural world and of all humanity. The earth signs are Taurus, Virgo and Capricorn; the air signs are Gemini, Libra and Aquarius; fire links Aries, Leo and Sagittarius; and Cancer, Scorpio and Pisces are identified with water. Earth signs are considered to be practical by nature, air signs intellectual, fire signs inspirational and water signs emotional.

When planning a project, you may find that the broad characteristics listed above will help you in your choice of colors and materials. Exploit the air of mystery surrounding the zodiac by working in richly textured fabrics, glowing metals and jewel-like colors enhanced with the gleam of gold. Decorate your creations with stars, the sun and moon, and the velvety deep blue of the night sky.

Above: A beautiful sixteenth-century astrological clock, from the Ducale Palace, Sala del Senato, Italy.

ASTROLOGICAL PIN CUSHION

An essential item on every Victorian dressing table, pin cushions are still as useful as they are decorative. There is no more appropriate way to personalize them than by using the pins themselves. The symbols for Capricorn and Taurus have been used here, but you will find templates for all the signs at the back of the book.

YOU WILL NEED

MATERIALS
plain velvet, 11 x 5½ in
brass-headed pins, ½ in long
matching sewing thread
fine white tissue paper
polyester batting

EQUIPMENT
scissors
tailor's chalk
sewing machine
sewing needle
pencil

1 Cut the velvet into two 5½ in squares and pin them together with right sides facing. Mark a ½ in seam allowance with tailor's chalk. Machine stitch around all four sides, leaving a 2 in opening in the center of one side.

2 Trim the seam allowance at the corners of the pin cushion and turn to right side, easing out the corners with the points of the scissors. Stuff very firmly with polyester batting. Sew up the opening neatly, by hand, along the seam line.

3 Trace the templates at the back of the book onto fine white tissue paper. Center and pin the motif onto the cushion.

4 Outline the motif with the pins. When done, tear away the tissue, pulling any stray bits from between the pins.

GILDED ZODIAC BOTTLE

Create a container fit for a magic potion using glowing glass paints to enhance a gilded design. This beautiful bottle would look stunning catching the light on a bathroom windowsill, but make sure the contents don't obscure the lovely jewel-like colors.

YOU WILL NEED

MATERIALS
flat-sided glass bottle
alcohol
gold glass-paint outliner pen
solvent-based glass paints: red,
  blue, green, yellow

EQUIPMENT
paintbrush

1 Wash the bottle thoroughly in hot water and dishwater detergent, then wipe with alcohol to remove any grease.

2 Practise using the gold outliner pen on paper before drawing the design (omitting the astrological signs) on one side of the bottle. Allow to dry for at least 24 hours.

3 Apply the glass paint between the outlines, brushing it on thickly to achieve an even coating. Leave the bottle on its side to dry for at least 24 hours.

4 Using the gold outliner pen, draw the astrological symbols around the design. Allow to dry completely before repeating the design on the other side of the bottle.

LIBRA EARRINGS

These delicate gold wire earrings take the form of tiny sets of scales. The miniature baskets are filled with beads in shades of green and blue, appropriate to the cool, balanced air sign of Libra. Be sure to thread the same number of beads into each basket so that the scales balance when you are wearing the earrings.

YOU WILL NEED

MATERIALS
one reel fine brass beading wire
selection of small glass beads in
  shades of blue and green
four jump rings
two split rings
one pair posts with loops
short length of 0.8 mm brass
  wire
one pair butterfly backs

EQUIPMENT
fine crochet hook
round-nosed pliers
round-ended pencil
wire cutters

1 With the fine wire, crochet four round shapes ½ in across. On the last round make three, ¾ in equally spaced loops. Leave a long end of wire. Twist the loops.

2 Mold each round into a dome shape with a pencil. Thread equal numbers of beads onto the loose end of wire and secure them in each basket. Do not trim the wire yet.

3 Using pliers, attach a jump ring, then a split ring, to each earring fitting. Cut two 1¾ in lengths of the thicker wire. Twist an upward loop in the center of each, then bend each end down into two loops from which the baskets will hang. Attach the center loop to the split ring using another jump ring. Thread the long end of wire on one basket through the top of the twisted loops to bring them together and attach to the bar. Repeat with the other baskets. Trim the ends of wire.

ZODIAC MOBILE

T o achieve the delicate balance of this ethereal mobile, you will need to cut the wire for the various shapes to the exact lengths given below.

YOU WILL NEED

MATERIALS
*2 mm, 1.6 mm and 1 mm,
 soft galvanized wire
medium-weight binding wire
aerosol spray paints: white
 primer, midnight blue, gold
nylon thread
curtain ring*

EQUIPMENT
*wire cutters
round-nosed pliers
thin cardboard or paper for
 templates
pen
flat-nosed pliers*

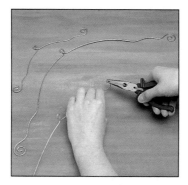

1 Use 2 mm wire for the hanging loops: cut one 30 in length and two 15 in lengths. Make a loop in the center of each and then secure with binding wire. Form waves and coils at each end using the round-nosed pliers.

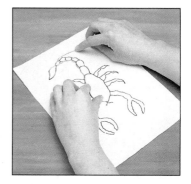

2 Trace the templates at the back of the book and copy the enlarged designs on the cardboard or paper. Form each motif by shaping the wire around the template. For the scorpion's body, use 26 in of 1.6 mm wire, binding the ends together at the head before trimming the excess. Cut two 13 in lengths of 1 mm wire for the claws, bend into shape and bind to the body, trimming the excess.

3 Following the scorpion template, use binding wire for the back legs and tail detail.

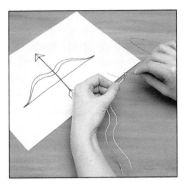

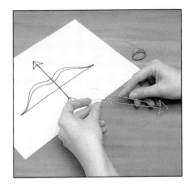

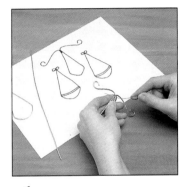

4 For Sagittarius, cut two 10 in lengths of 1.6 mm wire, bend into the bow shapes, and bind ends together, trimming excess and making the bowstring with binding wire.

5 Bend a 22 in length of 1 mm wire into an arrow shape, bind along the shaft and secure to the bow in the center.

6 For Libra, cut a 13½ in length of 2 mm wire for the balance bar. Bend into shape, coiling the ends into loops, and bind the two arms at the center. Cut two 9 in lengths of 1.6 mm wire for the scales. Bend into shape, using binding wire to outline the scales and bind to the bar.

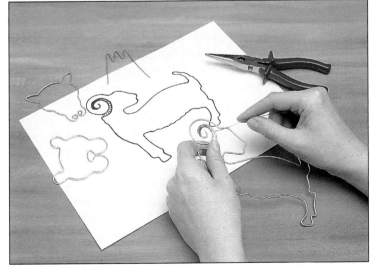

7 Follow the templates for Taurus, Leo, Aries and Pisces, binding where shown on the main picture and trimming excess wire. You will need the following lengths. Taurus: 13 in of 1.6 mm wire; the ½ in diameter ring is made from the same wire. Leo: 15 in of 1.6 mm wire; 8 in of 1 mm wire for the crown. Aries: 40 in of 1.6 mm wire. Pisces: 30 in of 1.6 mm wire.

8 Spray-paint the hanging loops and motifs with white primer and then paint them in the colors shown.

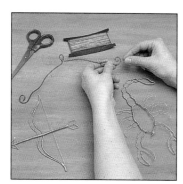

9 Assemble the mobile by attaching the shapes to the hanging loops with nylon thread (as shown in the main picture).

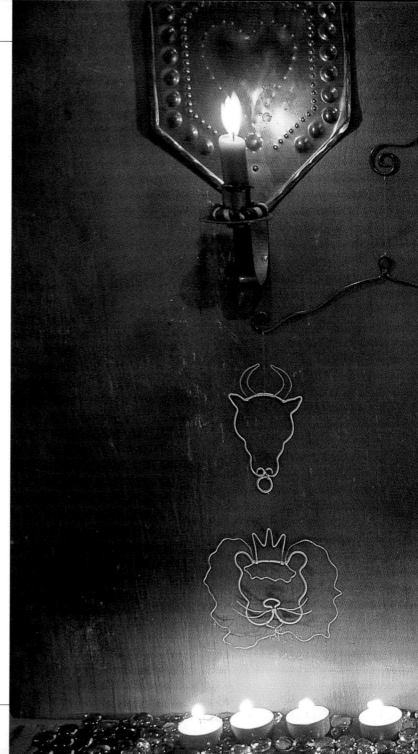

VELVET STAR-SIGN SCARF

This sinuous velvet scarf is encrusted down its full length with the sigils, or abstract symbols, of the twelve zodiac signs. The shiny metallic decorations contrast dramatically with the silky smooth fabric. Choose darkly glowing colors to wear on a starry evening. Before sewing the seams, make sure the pile of each piece of velvet is running in the right direction.

YOU WILL NEED

MATERIALS
velvet in main color,
*   60 in x 26 in*
velvet in contrasting color,
*   14 in x 26 in*
matching thread
metallic organza
matching embroidery floss

EQUIPMENT
scissors
tape measure
sewing machine
tailor's chalk
embroidery hoop
needle

1 Cut two 60 x 13 in lengths of velvet in main color, and four 7 x 13 in pieces of contrasting velvet. With right sides together and a ½ in seam allowance, machine stitch one contrasting panel to each end of each scarf length.

2 Mark out the positions for the astrological signs along the side of the scarf length, placing them ¾ in from the seam line and at about 5 in intervals. Using the templates at the back of the book, draw the symbols onto the velvet using tailor's chalk.

3 Place the velvet in an embroidery hoop. Cut ¾ in strips of metallic organza. Stitch one end of the organza to the marked line, twist the strip tightly and stitch in place. Work all the designs in the same way. With right sides together, join the two scarf lengths, leaving a small opening. Turn to the right side and slip-stitch the opening.

LEO LETTER RACK

This quaint letter rack, emblazoned with a confident lion, is just the thing to brighten up your desk. It is easy to assemble, and would make a ideal gift for a Leo friend's birthday.

YOU WILL NEED

MATERIALS
¼ in birch plywood sheet cut to just the following sizes:
  base 8½ in x 2⅞ in
  sides 5 in x 2⅞ in
  front 9 in x 4 in
  back 9in x 7½ in
wood glue
⅝ in wooden balls
white undercoat paint
acrylic paints: deep cobalt, deep yellow, cadmium red, gold, raw umber, black
matte varnish

EQUIPMENT
pen
ruler
pair of compasses
fret saw
sandpaper
masking tape
paintbrushes
stencil brush

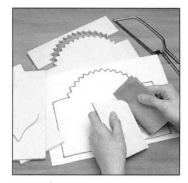

1 Mark out the back, front, base and two sides on the plywood to the sizes listed on the left. Use the template at the back of the book and cut out the back and sides. Cut out the other pieces and sand the edges.

2 Glue the pieces together and hold in place with tape until the glue has hardened completely. Remove the tape and sand all the edges and corners. Glue the wooden balls to the corners of the base.

3 Paint the letter rack with white undercoat, sanding down lightly when dry. With the stencil brush, stipple the rack with dark blue acrylic paint.

4 Complete the design in acrylic paints, using the main picture as a guide. Seal with a coat of matte varnish.

CANCER THE CRAB BROOCH

This delightful, glittering brooch is cleverly made from the humblest of materials: cardboard and newspaper.

YOU WILL NEED

MATERIALS
corrugated cardboard
newspaper
wallpaper paste
white glue
white acrylic primer
gouache paints: light blue,
  yellow, red
gloss varnish
gold enamel paint
brooch pin
epoxy resin glue

EQUIPMENT
scrap paper
pencil
craft knife
cutting mat
bowl
paintbrushes

1 Draw a star shape onto scrap paper and transfer the design onto the corrugated cardboard and cut out the star shape. Soak a piece of newspaper in wallpaper paste, scrunch it up and mound in the center of the star.

2 Cover the whole brooch in several layers of newspaper soaked in wallpaper paste. Allow to dry.

3 Give the brooch a coat of white glue, then one of white acrylic primer. Allow to dry, paint on the design and then the clear gloss varnish.

4 Add gold enamel paint details. Finally, fix a brooch pin to the back using epoxy resin glue.

STENCILED ZODIAC CURTAIN

Use gold fabric paints to dramatize a plain muslin curtain. Paint the shapes at random on the curtain, but try to plan your design so that they all appear frequently. Add variety by blending the two shades of gold on some of the designs you make.

YOU WILL NEED

MATERIALS
white muslin to fit window
fabric paints: light and
*   dark gold*
matching thread
curtain clips and metal rings

EQUIPMENT
tracing paper
pencil
stencil cardboard
craft knife
two stencil brushes
paper towels
newspaper
iron
masking tape
spray adhesive
saucers
sewing needle

1 Trace the stencil motifs from the back of the book and enlarge if necessary. Transfer onto 12 rectangles of stencil cardboard. Cut out the shapes using a craft knife. Before working on your curtain practice your stenciling technique on some spare fabric. Don't overload your brush and wipe off any excess paint on a paper towel before you begin.

2 Cover your work table with newspaper. Iron the muslin, then tape one corner to the table with masking tape, keeping it flat. Coat the back of each stencil lightly with spray adhesive before positioning it on the fabric. Start with the light gold, then paint over the edges of the motif with dark gold to give depth. Allow to dry, then gently peel the stencil off.

3 Cover the rest of the fabric with the motifs, repositioning it on the work table as necessary and stenciling one section at a time. Next, set the paint according to the manufacturer's instructions. Iron, then hem the edges, and attach the curtain clips to the upper edge.

PLANETARY WINDOW HANGING

Abstract astrological symbols are combined to create an original mobile, decorated with glass panels and beads which will catch the light as the pieces swing in the breeze.

YOU WILL NEED

MATERIALS
3 lb self-hardening modeling clay
five circles of 5 mm glass, 2 in diameter
one circle of 5 mm glass, 1¼ in diameter
0.8 mm copper wire, 4 in thin wire, 2 yd
glass beads in an assortment of colors and sizes
2 mm galvanized wire for hanging loop

EQUIPMENT
tracing paper
pencil
thin cardboard or paper
scissors
rolling pin
modeling tools
plastic bag
jewelry pliers
wire cutters
sewing needle
sandpaper

1 Trace the templates from the back of the book and transfer them onto thin cardboard or paper. Cut them out. Roll out the modeling clay to a flat sheet ¼ in thick.

2 Place one cutout shape on the clay sheet and cut around it with a modeling tool. Return excess clay to plastic bag to keep moist. With wet fingers, smooth all the surfaces and edges of the cutout shape.

3 Lift up the circular part of the shape and hold gently while positioning a circle of glass underneath (use the damp mark left by the clay on the work surface as a guide). Lower the clay and press it around the glass circle with wet fingers.

4 Cut out a circle of clay to reveal the glass, leaving a ⅛ in border.

5 Cut the copper wire in half and twist it into two small spirals using pliers. Press gently into the surface of the clay.

6 Use a needle to help you lift and position the colored glass beads and press them into the clay.

7 Pierce a small hole in the top and bottom of the piece and leave to dry. Repeat the process with the other shapes.

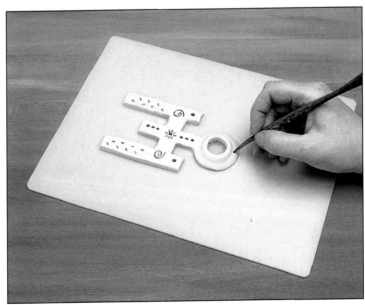

8 Once the pieces have fully dried and hardened, sand down all the edges.

9 Use thin wire to join the shapes together, and suspend from a wire loop.

GEMINI PAPER CUTOUTS

Gemini – the twins – is the chosen motif for this attractive cardboard decoration: the two halves of the cardboard are identical in design, yet one is the negative image of the other. Cutouts are traditional in Poland, where they are usually deftly cut freehand using just a pair of scissors.

YOU WILL NEED

MATERIALS
thin cardboard or paper in two colors, plus a large sheet for backing

EQUIPMENT
tracing paper
pencil
all-purpose glue
craft knife
cutting mat
scissors

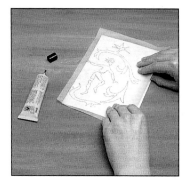

1 Trace the design from the template at the back of the book and enlarge if necessary. Attach the tracing to the rough side of one piece of colored cardboard with a little glue.

3 Remove the tracing paper and then turn the cardboard over, and back it with the contrasting color.

2 Using a craft knife, carefully cut out through the template and reserve all the shapes.

4 Cut the backing cardboard twice the size of the cutout cardboard. Fold it down the center. Stick a piece of the contrasting cardboard or paper to one side and arrange cutout pieces on it to match the original design. Stick the cutout cardboard on the opposite side.

PISCES HANGING ORNAMENTS

These charming little fish can be made quickly and would be a rewarding project for children to make. The symbol of Pisces represents coming and going, past and future, so when you hang these fish up, make them swim in different directions!

YOU WILL NEED

MATERIALS
scraps of woolen fabric
small mother-of-pearl buttons
  (two for each fish)
embroidery floss in two or three
  contrasting colors
scraps of polyester batting,
  approximately ¼ in thick

EQUIPMENT
scrap paper
pencil
thin cardboard or paper
  for template
scissors
pins
needle

1 Draw a fish motif onto scrap paper and transfer it onto thin cardboard or paper to make a template. Pin it to two layers of the fabric and cut out the fish (no seam allowance is required for these shapes).

2 Separate the pieces and sew on the buttons to make eyes. Embroider each side of the fish, using 3 strands of the embroidery floss, in cross stitch, stem stitch and feather stitch, as shown in the picture.

3 Cut a piece of batting using the template, then trim it so that it is slightly smaller all around than the fish.

4 Sandwich the wadding between the two sides, and attach some thread for the hanging loop. Blanket stitch the edges to join the sides together.

ASTROLOGICAL CLOCK

The passing of time is the basis of astrology; as the stars make their regular journeys around the heavens, you can reflect on time's importance with the help of this stylish clock. Battery-operated clock mechanisms are now readily available; all you have to supply is the clock face.

YOU WILL NEED

MATERIALS
sheet of thick white cardboard
set of zodiac signs
black acrylic paint
quartz clock with hands

EQUIPMENT
scissors
pair of compasses
pencil
craft knife
white glue
paintbrush

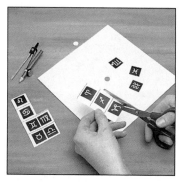

1 Cut a square of card measuring 8 in. Draw a circle slightly smaller than the square. Cut out a small circle in the center of the cardboard to fit where the hands meet. Photocopy a set of zodiac symbols, or draw your own using the templates at the back of this book. Cut them out.

2 Arrange the 12 star signs around the clock face, in the correct order (as shown in the picture). Position those corresponding to 12, 3, 6 and 9 o'clock first, then space the rest equally. Stick down with white glue.

3 Paint the area around the clock face black. Allow the paint to dry, then seal the whole clock with two coats of diluted white glue. Attach the internal mechanism and the hands. Insert a battery.

CANCER THE CRAB PLAQUE

This engaging crab plaque is easily made from molded papier-mâché. To make paper pulp, soak small pieces of newspaper in water overnight. Boil it until paper disintegrates, whisk to a pulp with a fork, then squeeze out any water in a sieve. Mix with white glue or dry wallpaper paste with a few drops of oil of cloves.

YOU WILL NEED

MATERIALS
strong cardboard
wire for hanging
masking tape
newspaper
wallpaper paste
paper pulp
white latex paint
self-hardening clay
acrylic or poster paints:
  turquoise blue, navy blue,
  pink, yellow
gloss varnish

EQUIPMENT
scissors
wire cutters
clay modeling tool
paintbrushes

1 Cut a piece of cardboard about 5 in square. Cut a short piece of wire and bend into a hook. Attach to one side of the cardboard with tape.

2 Soak 1 in squares of newspaper in wallpaper paste and apply to both sides of the card. When dry, apply paper pulp to the border area. Allow to dry thoroughly.

3 Apply a coat of latex emulsion. When dry, use self-hardening clay to make relief decorations and frame, shaping them with a modeling tool. Leave to harden.

4 Paint crab and border in acrylic or poster paints. Seal with several coats of varnish.

TAURUS GIFT WRAP

Personalize a special birthday gift by creating original gift wrap stenciled with the relevant star-sign. A deep red and black have been used here to match the energetic, earthy character of the Taurean. Be careful not to overload the brush when stenciling; blot any excess paint on a paper towel before you begin. If paint does seep under the edges of the stencil, wipe it off carefully before repositioning the acetate.

YOU WILL NEED

MATERIALS
plain deep red gift wrap
black acrylic paint

EQUIPMENT
pencil
thin cardboard or paper
 for template
sheet of acetate
permanent black pen
craft knife
cutting mat
masking tape
stencil brush

1 Draw a template following the finished picture and transfer it onto cardboard or paper. Place the acetate over the template and trace the outline with a black pen.

2 Carefully cut out the stencil using a craft knife.

3 Decide on the positioning of the motifs on the paper, marking lightly with a pencil if necessary. Position the stencil and use a little masking tape to hold it in place. Stipple the design with the stencil brush. Lift the stencil off carefully and repeat to cover the paper.

WATER-BEARER PLAQUE

Aquarius the water-bearer carries the waters of creation and symbolizes death and renewal. This charming wall plaque is made of molded papier-mâché. You will find the recipe for making paper pulp on page 40.

YOU WILL NEED

MATERIALS
corrugated cardboard
masking tape
paper pulp
newspaper
wallpaper paste
white glue
white acrylic primer
gouache paints: pale blue,
* dark blue, orange, deep red*
gloss varnish
gold enamel paint
mirror-hanging hook
epoxy resin glue

EQUIPMENT
pencil
thin cardboard or
* paper for templates*
craft knife
cutting mat
bowl
paintbrushes

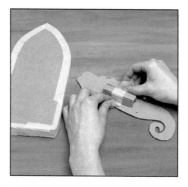

1 Draw templates for the plaque, its sides and figure, and transfer to corrugated cardboard. Cut out and assemble with masking tape. Make a small "step" from cardboard and fix to the figure's back.

2 Apply paper pulp to the front of the figure to give it a rounded shape. When dry, cover the figure and plaque in several layers of newspaper pieces soaked in wallpaper paste. Leave to dry.

3 Paint on a coat of white glue followed, when dry, by a coat of white acrylic primer. Decorate the plaque and figure with gouache paints.

4 Varnish, then, when dry, highlight details with gold enamel paint. With epoxy resin glue, secure the figure and fix a mirror-hanging plate to the back.

SCORPIO PLATE

For this papier-mâché plate, the color is incorporated into the paper pulp before it is molded. See page 40 for a recipe for paper pulp. This would be a great project for a family to make, with each person making their own sign.

YOU WILL NEED

MATERIALS
acrylic paints
paper pulp
strong cardboard
white glue
crepe paper
wallpaper paste
white pencil or chalk
black latex paint (optional)
gold paint (optional)

EQUIPMENT
fork
pencil
plate
craft knife
cutting mat
tracing paper
thin cardboard or paper
 for template
paintbrush (optional)

1 Using a fork, stir acrylic paint into the paper pulp until the color is evenly mixed. Cut out 2 circles of cardboard the same size (use an old plate as a template). Cut a smaller circle from one, and then glue the rim to the front of the other circle and the center to the back. Cover with crepe paper soaked in wallpaper paste.

2 Press colored pulp onto the edge of the plate, building it up in thin layers, and adding more when dry. Trace the scorpion template from the back of the book and transfer to thin card or paper. Cut it out and draw around it with chalk or white pencil onto the plate. Build up the body with pulp, covering the outline.

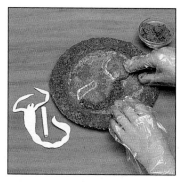

3 Add finer details such as legs and claws with more thin layers of paper pulp. Allow to dry completely. To add definition, take a dry brush with a little black latex and wipe lightly over scorpion and rim of plate. Repeat with gold paint.

Embroidered Scented Leo Cushion

T his regal cushion is fit for the kingly lion. When stuffing the cushion, you can either scent the batting with a few drops of essential oil, or tuck a small amount of potpourri in with the stuffing.

You Will Need

Materials
cream cotton (such as sheeting), 9 in square
interfacing, 9 in square
embroidery floss: black and 5 graduated shades of yellow and gold
dark blue velvet, 13 x 6½ in
matching thread
gold cord, 15 in
polyester toy batting
essential oil or potpourri
four gold tassels

Equipment
tracing paper
pencil
transfer pen or dressmaker's carbon
needle
embroidery hoop
iron
scissors

1 Trace the template at the back of the book and transfer the design onto the cotton fabric. Baste the interfacing to the back and mount in a hoop. Using two strands of embroidery thread, work the two circles in split stitch in dark gold, then outline the lion and zodiac symbols in black, using straight and split stitch. Fill in the background with long and short stitches, blending the colors from light to dark gold.

3 Cut the velvet into two 6½ in squares. Tack then stitch the motif to the center front of one square. Slip-stitch the gold cord around the circle. Make a small slit in the velvet and push the two ends to the wrong side. Sew over the slit. Pull out the basting threads.

2 Remove the hoop and press the embroidery lightly on the wrong side. Cut out, leaving a ¼ in seam allowance. Clip the curves and baste the seam allowance to the back.

4 With right sides facing each other, sew 3 sides together. Secure the corners and turn. Fill with batting (and potpourri if using). Slip-stitch the opening, and sew a tassel to each corner.

CANCER THE CRAB BOX

This attractive little box would make a delightful present in itself, or could be used to house a special gift. The lid is painted in a wavy pattern inspired by the crab's watery home and dotted with stars to underline its astrological significance.

YOU WILL NEED

MATERIALS
⅜ x 1¼ in pine slats, cut into 4
    4 in lengths
⅛ in birch plywood sheet, cut into
    the following sizes:
    base and lid insert: 3¼ x 4 in
    lid: 4½ x 4 in
    crab motif: 4 x 4 in
wood glue
white undercoat paint
acrylic paints: deep cobalt,
    deep yellow, cadmium red,
    gold, raw umber, black
matte varnish

EQUIPMENT
fret saw
pencil
tracing paper
sandpaper
masking tape
paintbrushes

1 Cut out the four pine slats and a base, lid and lid insert from the plywood. Trace the crab template from the back of the book and transfer it to the plywood. Cut it out and sand off any rough edges.

2 Assemble the sides of the box with wood glue and hold in place with masking tape until the glue is dry. Glue in the base. Glue the lid insert to the center of the lid. Sand down any rough corners and edges.

3 Paint the box and crab with a coat of white undercoat. Sand lightly when dry. Paint the box and lid with the blue base color, watered down and applied with a wavy brush stroke. Paint on border pattern and stars. Paint crab in red, and highlight details in blue and gold. Finish off with a coat of matte varnish. Glue the crab firmly onto the lid of the box.

CELESTIAL MAP MIRROR

The zodiac stands for the changing of the seasons as the sun appears to circle the earth, and astrologers draw it as a circle, with each of the twelve sections presided over by its familiar sign. Here, the ancient calendar is the inspiration for a striking engraved frame. Secure the hook firmly to the back of the frame to support the weight of the mirror.

YOU WILL NEED

MATERIALS
2¼ lb self-hardening
 modeling clay
⅛ in thick circular mirror,
 cut to 6 in in diameter
acrylic paints: deep turquoise,
 white, lemon yellow, purple
matte varnish
plate-hanging fixture

EQUIPMENT
plate
pencil
thin cardboard or paper
rolling pin
modeling tools
paintbrushes
epoxy resin glue

1 Draw around a plate onto thin cardboard or paper to make a template. Roll out the clay to a large flat sheet ¼ in thick. Cut two circles of clay.

2 Place the mirror on one of the circles and cut around it. Fit the mirror between the two frames, stretching the clay over the mirror's edge.

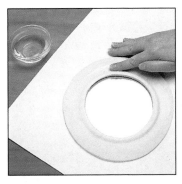

3 Secure the frame by pressing down through both layers with wet fingers at intervals around the outer edge, then smooth the inner and outer edges to leave a neat finish.

4 Trim the inner edge of the frame to leave an overlap of ¼ in around the mirror. Neaten with a modeling tool.

▶

5 Wet and smooth the surface, then divide into twelve equal sections by engraving straight lines with a wet modeling tool from the raised inner border to the edge of the frame.

6 Engrave an astrological sign in each section of the frame, following the correct order shown in the photograph. Allow to harden completely.

7 Mix turquoise, white and lemon acrylic paint, adding water to achieve a creamy consistency, and paint the frame in two thin coats, allowing the brush strokes to show through. Allow the first coat to dry before applying the second.

8 Mix purple and white paint, this time to a thicker texture, and apply with a wide dry brush so that the engraved figures and raised inner edge remain green. When dry, coat with one layer of clear varnish and attach the hook to the back with epoxy resin glue.

SAGITTARIUS TILE

The subtle, antiqued look of this unique tile is achieved very simply by staining it with tea. Wiping the design with color accentuates the relief and you can keep staining until the shade is the intensity you desire.

YOU WILL NEED

MATERIALS
*1 lb self-hardening modeling clay
matte varnish*

EQUIPMENT
*tracing paper
pencil
rolling pin
modeling tools
tea bag
paintbrush*

1 Trace and enlarge the template at the back of the book. Roll out the clay to a flat sheet ½ in thick.

2 Place the tracing on top of the clay and mark all the lines using a modeling tool.

3 Wet the clay surface thoroughly to make it easier to manipulate. Indent the lines of the design, molding the figure's body to raise it above the background area.

▶

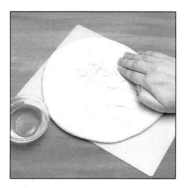

4 Smooth the surface with wet fingers as you work to keep the clay moist.

5 Cut out the tile shape and engrave a double border around the edge to frame the central motif.

6 Stipple the background with the point of a wet modeling tool to create texture. Then leave the tile to harden completely before staining.

7 Brew a strong cup of tea with a tea bag and use to stain the clay, wiping over the design with the tea bag. When you are satisfied with the color, leave the tile to dry, then protect it with a coat of matte varnish.

TEMPLATES

To enlarge the templates to the correct size, use either a grid system or a photocopier. For the grid system, trace the template and draw a grid of evenly spaced squares over your tracing. To scale up, draw a larger grid onto another piece of paper. Copy the outline onto the second grid by taking each square individually and drawing the relevant part of the outline in the larger square. Finally, draw over the lines to make sure they are continuous.

Astrological Pin Cushion p. 12

Gemini Paper Cutouts p. 34

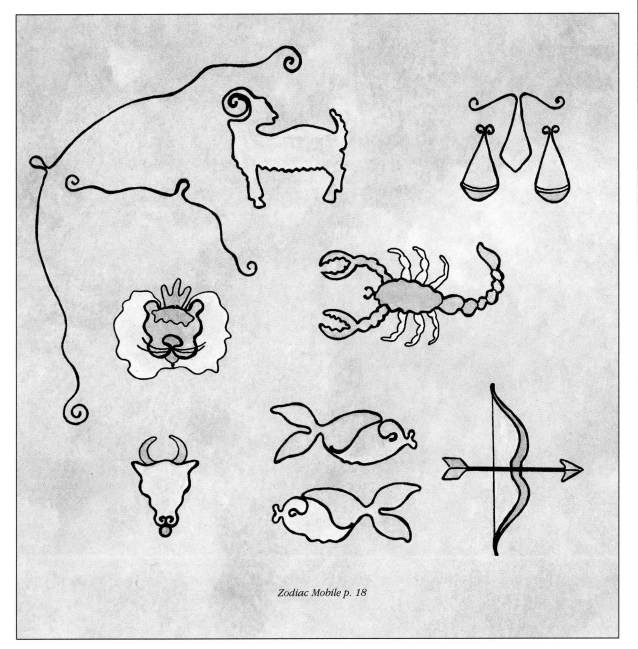

Zodiac Mobile p. 18

Stenciled Zodiac Curtain p. 28

Leo Letter Rack p. 24

Scorpio Plate p. 46

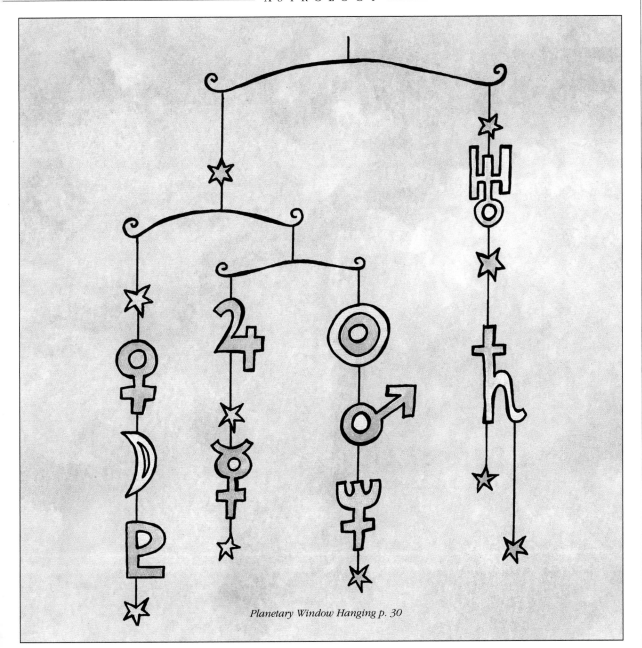

Planetary Window Hanging p. 30

Cancer the Crab Box p. 50

Embroidered Scented Leo Cushion p. 48

Sagittarius Tile p. 55

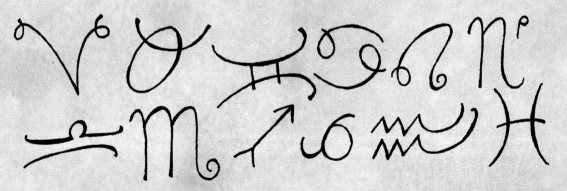

Velvet Star-sign Scarf p. 22

ACKNOWLEDGMENTS

The author and publishers would like to thank the following people for designing the projects in this book:

Ofer Acco

Planetary Window Hanging p. 30; Celestial Map Mirror p. 53; Sagittarius Tile p. 55.

Amanda Blunden

Cancer the Crab Plaque p. 40.

Penny Boylan

Astrological Pin Cushion p. 12; Pisces Hanging Ornaments p. 36.

Louise Brownlow

Libra Earrings p. 16; Gemini Paper Cutouts p. 34; Scorpio Plate p. 46.

Lucinda Ganderton

Stenciled Zodiac Curtain p. 28; Embroidered Scented Leo Cushion p. 48.

Dawn Gulyas

Zodiac Mobile p. 18.

Jill Hancock

Leo Letter Rack p. 24; Cancer the Crab Box p. 50.

Emma Petitt

Gilded Zodiac Bottle p. 14.

Kim Rowley

Cancer the Crab Brooch p. 26; Water-Bearer Plaque p. 44.

Isabel Stanley

Velvet Star-sign Scarf p. 22.

Josephine Whitfield

Astrological Clock p. 38; Taurus Gift Wrap p. 42.

Picture Credits
The Publishers would like to thank the following picture libraries for permission to use their pictures on pages:
AKG, London: p. 10, p. 11 (bottom right). E.T Archive, London: p. 8 (bottom), p. 9, p. 11 (top left). Visual Arts Library: p. 8 (top left).